No Father

Julene Tripp Weaver

Plain View Press
P.O. 42255
Austin, TX 78704

plainviewpress.net
pk@plainviewpress.net
512-441-2452

Copyright © 2011 Julene Tripp Weaver. All rights reserved under International and Pan-American Copyright Conventions. No part of this book may be reproduced or distributed in any form or by any means, or stored in a data base or retrieval system, without written permission from the author. All rights, including electronic, are reserved by the author and publisher.

ISBN: 978-1-935514-80-0
Library of Congress Control Number: 2010942409

Front Cover Art: *She Walks Slowly-Attempting to Disappear into Anonymity as the Wind Blows Heavy with Lament, the Buildings Dance to a Sorrowful Beat, and Sidewalks Run Thick With the Blood of Those Who Can No Longer Sing,* © 2009 By Duane Kirby Jensen, 16" x 20", acrylic on Deep Edge Canvas

Back Cover Art: *New love and last days goes unnoticed,* © 2010 by Duane Kirby Jensen, 16" x 20", acrylic on panel

To see more of his art, please visit: artofduanekirbyjensen.com

Cover design by Susan Bright

Contents

Section I: Girl Wonders — 7

Teaspoons	9
You Will Not Bring Home Jesus Christ	10
Out In the World	11
Eat Your Vegetables	12
Dark Shadows	13
Recipes To Make a Submissive	15
Double Dutch Date	18
Swing Street Secrets, 1968	19
Family Going Down	21
Deeper Than Wild	22
Flashers	23
A Pink Carnation For Daddy, But I Want Red	24
Mother's Suitors	25
Beginning To Understand	26
History Hardened In My Brain	27
Plain Jane	28
Men Running Things	29
What We Lose Finds Us	30
Sixteen, Aching For Life	31
Holding Onto Her Past	32
Girls Like Her	33
Love Fest On Bleecker Street	34

Section II: Female Festers — 37

Anything, To Take Away the Pain	39
Mama You Just Don't Know	40
What Can a Street Urchin Expect?	42
Abandonment To Pleasure	43
Ideal Childhood Except For Hodgkin's Cancer	45
One Of the Many	46
The Other Side	47
And If There Is No God	48
The Expert	49
Truant	50
Ivory Coast Boy	52
Lessons From a Surrogate	53
What Is Buried and Past	54
Pastoral Landscape	55
Feral	56

Myths Of Difference	57
Infatuation	58
Freak	59
Chevy Impala '60	60
Breakfast Special	61
Sunday Morning	62
Union	63
Paint Job	65
Catalyst To Manhattan	67
A Good Arrangement	68
Smell Of Mother	70

Section III: Woman Stands   71

Pushed Edges: Lovemap Explorations	73
Spice Rack	75
Hot Woman	77
I. Safety Fable	78
II. Beyond the School for Wayward Girls	78
III. Jesus Tossed The Dice	79
One End To the Other	80
St. Mark's Place Brother	81
Snared	83
Meant To Be	84
My Brave Lynx	86
Salvatore's	87
Love Transformations	89
The Only Thing Left	93
Birthday Reflection	94
All I Want	95
Hot Days Of Past	96
Cupcake	97
A Family Visit	98
Fruit Fly Song	99
Family Endurance	100
Ice Storm, Early 1950s	101
About the Author	103

Acknowledgements

Acknowledgments and thanks go to the following publications in which some of the poems in this collection previously appeared, sometimes in earlier versions: *Chicken Pinata* for "Chevy Impala '60" and "My Brave Lynx." *Clara Venus* for "Love Transformations" (accepted, as "After Twenty-Two Years"). *Gemini Magazine* for "You Will Not Bring Home Jesus Christ." *Hot Metal Press* for "Ice Storm, Early 1950s." *Knock* for "Pastoral Landscape." *Las Cruces Poets & Writers Magazine* and *Letters to the World*, Poems from the Wom-Po Listserv for "A Family Visit." *Nerve Cowboy* for "Family Going Down." *Penitalia* for "Flashers" and "Hot Woman." *Pocket Slut* for "Abandonment To Pleasure." *Pilgrimage Magazine* For "Swing Street Secrets, 1968." *Redheaded Stepchild* for "St. Mark's Place Brother." *Riverbabble* for "Snared." *Qarrtsiluni* for "One of the Many." *Under a Silver Sky, An Anthology of Pacific Northwest Poetry* for "Paint Job."

For chapbook size manuscripts of this book, I thank Susan Slaviero, editor at *Blossombones* for notifying me my manuscript was a finalist in their Chapbook Contest. Also, thanks to Lana Hechtman Ayers, editor at *Concrete Wolf*, for Honorary Mention in their Chapbook Contest. A special thank you to Lana for her endless assistance and sister support. She gave me the faith to believe I would publish, first a chapbook, then a full-size book.

I appreciate the retreat at the University of Washington's Helen Riaboff Whitely Center to work on my writing.

For constant support through the years and insightful feedback I thank Deborah Woodard, Elizabeth Austen, Lana Hechtman Ayers, Kayt Hoch, Holly Thomas, Suzanne Edison, Fredda Jaffe, Ruth Bavetta, and Nina Bennett.

Also, I am grateful to Susan Bright at *Plain View Press* for her selection of my manuscript and her work to help bring it to fruition. And, my appreciation to Duane Kirby Jensen for his colorful art which graces the covers. Much appreciation to Michael Schein for his stellar legal expertise, and, to Lori A. May for her proofreading skills.

Last, but most important, this book would not be possible if not for the support of my life partner John Perkins. To him, an extra special thank you, with love.

Section I

Girl Wonders

All things appear to us as they appear to us, and it is impossible for them to appear otherwise.

—*Umberto Eco*

Teaspoons

Special permission child,
a rare visit to Dad at the Albany Veterans
Hospital. A slow walk, each room

its own tablet of unknown story.
My dad's room a dose of sorrow
I cannot swallow.

Always a smile for his little girl.
His bone thin arms hold me
against his hard chest.

We will go to the World's Fair,

his story.
I swallow with a smile.
A waterfall crashes inside me.

We stare at the clock tower outside.
My life makes me tired,
so full of its teaspoons of death.

You Will Not Bring Home Jesus Christ

to my house
unless it *is* Jesus Christ.
No one better go near you.
Watch out for that Greek boy,
that Italian boy
that Jewish boy.
Boys look like kittens
but turn into tigers.
Don't look at them.
Don't stare.
Don't go out alone.
Don't write poetry.
Be a nurse, a teacher, a secretary,
so after you marry and your man leaves
you can start over.

Out In the World

At twelve, she's wise to it already,
that any man would have her.
She imagines she'd like a man
hard, angles of bone, firm muscles
to come into her—male grit, heat.

When she plays
in the playground, late after school,
where shadows grow long,
her basketball keeps missing the hoop.
She knows in her soft gut
she should go home when a man slows his car
calls to her, Hello, pretty.
She looks up, her face red,
her skirt too short, the night swirls
in between her legs. She says
Hi. And the man speaks again, *Want*
> *to see what I have?*
> *Come closer,*
> *you sure are pretty.*

She inches forward, being polite,
stands at the car window, notices movement like a ball
he dribbles, his hand rapid in his lap.
She knows this is what everyone warns her about,
he is one of those men who do bad things.
She runs home, never tells.

Eat Your Vegetables

She sits, stares out the kitchen window
toward the lake out past the trees
summer on its way to full bloom
water will turn from blue to green algae soon.

Eat your vegetables, her mother says.
She prefers to go outside, cross the thicket to the lake.
She wants to toss stones,
to sit and stare at the ripples she creates.

Eat your vegetables.
She plays with dull green string beans from a can,
mixes beet juice with the white potatoes,
soaks the dry pork chop—
against the turquoise kitchen table.

She longs to feel the soft mud
in the still blue reflected lake.
She takes another bite,
weaves a blanket story of some poor girl
who longs for a mother with imagination.

Eat your vegetables, the mother repeats.
She stuffs her face so she can cross the thicket
to the lake.

Dark Shadows

Daddy drove home
daily at four-thirty.
I ran to his car, his welcome hug
from my favorite renegade show,
Dark Shadows—the one Mother
did not allow me to watch. Ran to Daddy
from the daily fights I always won.

Home from Monticello,
the racetrack town, where Uncle
played the horses. An accountant,
Daddy kept the books for an air
conditioning firm. *The big Borsht Belt*
    hotels have to upgrade to survive,
    Mother said.

We drove up Swiss Hill
to Grandma's farm
past the resort that burnt to the ground,
then the one still standing, with tennis courts,
a big ballroom—where
stars from the city, like Bing Crosby,
sang wooing love songs.

I crawled through those fields
once, on my knees to avoid the bulls,
escaping from Mother. Daddy found me,
scooped me into his arms, said, *Your mother*
is worried about you. Let's go home now.
No. My tears into his cotton shirt.
    But we must go home your mother loves you.

No she doesn't.

She does, just like I do.
And he took me home.
But where was I to go
after his funeral,
after Grandma's farm was sold.

Recipes To Make a Submissive

"To cream: ...Press the mixture in a gentle gliding motion... in short rocking strokes, over a rather limited area..."
>Joy of Cooking, Volume 2
>by Irma S. Rombauer & Marion Rombauer Becket

I lie in my bed
after Sunday school
dreaming stained-glass visions
of a sweet shepherd boy—
such beautiful
blond hair. I long
to save him from his fate,
sacrifice whatever it is I have.
My fingers idle
between my thighs.

Mother layers dense coconut cream
between white round cakes.
She licks her long lean fingers
whispers—
>Men only want one thing.

One thing—
        what?

Dole canned pineapple and
maraschino cocktail cherries,
I'm not supposed to eat. My fingers
sticky sweet, place each cherry
carefully in the center
upside-down perfection.

She teaches me to soften
butter, press the spoon
hard into the grains of sugar
rub them against the side of the bowl.
She guides my hands, harder,
tells me—

> *When women grow old*
> > *men don't want them anymore.*

This can't be true—
    can it?

Under direction
I top Ritz crackers
with salami, cheddar,
small masterpieces of perfection.
Mom slices olives,
carefully so the centers
don't fall out.

Pink-sweet strawberry chiffon pie,
Mom cuts perfect triangle wedges
measured for company.
She tells me—
> *Never take your pants down*
> > *for any boy.*

I wonder—
    why?

Her belly grows large
between her and the table.
She sits me on the edge
of her bed, explains birth
control, how she carefully
planned this eight-year separation
between me and my coming
baby sister.

> *Slide the diaphragm inside*
> > *place it flat.*

Flat—
    over what?

I could help bake a cake
for that blond boy
make him celery boats
topped with pretty pimentos.
I knead harder
between my thighs.
Face-to-face with my savior,
I believe in miracles.

Double Dutch Date

One of those
go-nowhere
        no-money
                back-seat of a car
                        fixed-up blind dates.

We pool all our cash
        for a six-pack
drive down to the river
sit on large cool rocks.

Water bubbles in the dark.
The other couple wanders downstream.
Alone, we sit in silence
listen to pebbles talk.

Our hands idle close.
We give in to the pull
of a bittersweet
beer-breath kiss.

If Mom finds out
        I'll be grounded for days.

The river, our puppy dog kisses,
our soft hugs quiet my fear.
I fall into a river of desire, once
        wet, I discover water dries.

How easy it is to lie.
Name some movie, a girlfriend
not mention my Double Dutch date
or the river I hold tight
                in my pocketed heart.

Swing Street Secrets, 1968

Out with Uncle,
dapper we walk
         West 52nd Street.
He's sharp in his long detective overcoat.

Jazz beats strum airwaves.
         Words float on smoke.
A dance inside me trapped
         in my new black pumps.

     This street is hard-core, he says.
         Nice girls don't come here alone.

         He ushers me into his favorite bar…

Adults whisper secrets
         in darkened rooms
                  their heads tilt back.

Uncle's wild past a rumor to decipher—
black and white photos I've stared at all my life.
         He stands tall, chest out, a girl on each arm—
                  the sweet one he never married.

He steps away to the bar.
     Don't leave with anyone, I'll be back.

The black boy didn't interest me
     but the chance to dance
     make up my own mind.
I knew taboo, but he asked.
And oh, to dance on that hard wood floor
with everyone dancing, I had to answer
the answer had to be yes.

Fun stops sudden as a slap. Uncle
        pulls hard on my arm, *It's time to go.*
                I say, *No.*
We three a spectacle bouncers surround.
        Tearing with apology I exit the floor.
My black pumps pulse stoic jazzed with dance
        to my core. I walk Swing Street
                secrets tall.

Family Going Down

Uncle: Belly-big you stand in smoke, barbeque
a steak, stuff all the faces to feed. You used to
be a steam-rolling sex machine. In dress-up you
were debonair: Pressed pants, in your faulty body,
one leg an inch shorter than the other, bulging muscles
from chopping wood. Perhaps you had one too many
girlfriends and never could decide which one was
enough like your mom who you cared for till she died.

Now each woman you meet is unworthy.
You fuck some, others you sit, watch TV
alongside their mother. And if there's a kiss inside you
when you lean in toward her, voices come out of the
dark, and you forget what the love of a woman
could ever mean. You put your life on hold.
Drink to drown the voices. Pray in tongues
while your sister takes Baptism when she
hits fifty. Finally, you give up even trying
to decide. Life is all it really is.

Still, the photos show the young man inside.
Fighting with sister you know your blood
pressure is rising, the oldest teen is
out fucking like a slut gone bad, and you
courted her till she ran away—
now all that's left is death coming, knocking out
one family member after the other.

Deeper Than Wild

He spoiled my future for the normal.
Dutiful in his Uncle role
written in some family book he read,
he took over when his sister's husband died.

Dutiful in his Uncle role
lessons he taught me, lessons I learned.
He triumphed when Daddy died,
deadly secrets of his wild days.

Lessons learned, he taught me:
Never drink three Manhattans. They'll put you under the table.
I knew Uncle had wild days. Deadly secrets.
The old Metropolitan, midtown.

Three Manhattans put me under the table:
night life, party hats, noise makers,
the old Metropolitan, midtown
champagne toast at midnight when I was all but thirteen.

Night life, party hats, noisemakers
instructions in some family book he read,
champagne toast with Uncle, New Year's at thirteen
spoiling my future for the normal.

Flashers

They were on the periphery
like telephone poles.
I walked past.

In subway stations,
I walked toward the middle
where there were more people.
Such characters hang out at the far ends.

I never reported them to the police,
didn't even think this possible.
But they are burrowed inside my cells,
these exposed men with erect penises,
open coats, no pants, wanting
their privates witnessed.

A Pink Carnation For Daddy, But I Want Red

When you were alive,
a father full-fledged,
when you tobogganed
down the hill, wrapping me
in your arms, shouting your joy,
your smile was a cup
overflowing from my heart.

The empty days without you,
the dredged sorrow
of your funeral that hot August.
My tears. The sky empty
as the eyes of my mother,
who carried the red carnation
to throw on your grave that day.

I had to be watered down,
had to throw the pink carnation.
I ran and ran to the lake,
  Daddy I miss you.
The clear water was still.

Mother's Suitors

—after Belle Waring

Dad had narrow lips, good for kissing.
He licked frosting off the edge of a knife
at a birthday party once.
Half the guests declined the cake.
I ate doubles of leftovers,
sweet lunch for days.

Dad was a short man, inches shorter
than my mother, handsome in their wedding album.
Uncle's notable absence, one of our many family secrets.

Dad's death was slow by starvation.
His lips hardened with Hodgkin's cancer.
Uncle won his war, got his sister back
forever, till death did they part.
Dad was always expendable according to Uncle,
our puffed up family rooster.

Uncle was a large man, self-inflicted caregiver
to succulent ancestors of our dying family.
Me, I like to lick the sharp edges.

Our family has no sophisticated habits.
First Dad, then Uncle
showed me this world.
Still there are large cuts. I insist
I'll slice my own.

Beginning To Understand

Called to the bath I hesitate,
my mother's elongated flat breasts
repel me.   She is taller than my
small dad.   Two blocks that do not fit.
I run to the lake in the back of our house,
a place where voices say, forget bodies,
a favorite wide rooted tree to lean against.

Always we travel to visit Mother's family
in the city,   trapped with nowhere to escape
from this woman who made me,   the sweet
smell of bus exhaust   my antidote
to a world changed.   Dad's death
shifts everything.   Upstate, old fishermen
slide their hands down my mother's shirt.

She insists a fitting for a bra.   Sends me alone
to Macy's in Queens.   A matronly saleswoman
adjusts the straps, coaches me to bend over,
shake-in, for a perfect fit. Her hands sure guides,
my body exposed, stiff-still 'till she leaves,
then, I hold myself high in white-peaked wonder.

Mother has checked out, we move to her childhood
home with her brother   my new dad.
She's deader than dead.   Her breasts still hang low
in water. Don't expect anything in this life, she tells me,
come, run the water for my bath.

History Hardened In My Brain

> *The Basement: Meditations on a Human Sacrifice,*
> based on the death of Sylvia Likens,
> an installation by Kate Millet, 1978

Sylvia was my age, sixteen.
I dragged my little sister,
to see Kate's installation.

We stared at Sylvia's
papier-mâché body
burnt and bruised on a bare
dirt-sodden mattress—

Sylvia was thrown
into the basement with the dogs,
her thin teen body beaten,
burned with cigarettes, starved
till she died. *I am a prostitute
and proud of it!* carved
on her soft belly.

We listened to the drone of
court hearings looped in the
background. Only four avengers
on trial. Her foster mother's voice,
a low whimper, *I was too doped up
      to know what was going on.*
Her daughter's voice breaking in a sob,
      *Yes, it was my mother
who carved the first word on Sylvia.*

We are Sylvia Likens.

Plain Jane

Always a plain Jane
the dork in the oversized plaid skirt
knee-high socks and penny loafers sans
any coin, my hair stood on end cowlick.
City country girl—the hip kids razed me over,
caught me picking my nose. If those had been
healthy times, the wholesome embroidered
fabric absorbing dirt from the crevices—
if only the grains fell into place a happy
everything—a father still intact fast forwarded
to a future where Hodgkin's cancer had a cure
a future world beyond the death
of Kennedy or MLK. But all that everything
too much to even hope for. The skirt got a
blood stain that never washed out. There were
never enough answers back in the past for a plain
Jane bewildered, wondering what her story might
ever turn into.

Men Running Things

Men work: stand around at construction sites
between orange cones, cement blocks: they sit
on building ledges: eat giant subs: watch women.

They spend countless hours figuring out next
steps. They dig, plow, shuffle buckets of earth,
create a hole, use cranes: move concrete blocks

and mortar one square meter to the next: plaster walls
into the sky. They stand in the sun their skin cracked
like dry earth craters. They have fondling eyes

for every pair of breasts. We walk past them tempering
our heel clicks, hyperaware our jiggles entertain them.
They cat call, "Hey babe, what you doing tonight?"

We notice their muscles in strong arms: easy to
sling fifty pound sacks of concrete: know
they have a wife, kids. There's that lingering

rescue fantasy: these brawny bronze muscle-
tempered males, so physical, they can crack
the back of any man who would bring you down.

The history of female: make your man breakfast
before he heads off to work: our power subtle—
male monsters ingest our love: go off to construct.

What We Lose Finds Us

I could have been at Woodstock.
Yasger's Farm an easy stretch down the road
from Grandma's, the era of Haight-Ashbury,
hippies plastered *Life*, *Newsweek*, and *Time*.

Those kids might camp in our barn,
burn it to the ground, Uncle's gritted teeth
determination to protect his land.
I want to go too. Radio idols, rock n' roll.

Blues in my ear, I dream Hendrix
live—catch a shred of his smashed guitar.
Too young, Uncle declares. Radio reports of
road blocks, no one can get through.

He bribes me, a five for a quart of milk, and,
Keep the change. I return—he made his
get-away. Clean-cut citizen, property owner,
ushered easily past police blockades.

I wail.
        Pound walls.
                Cry.

Hippie earring chick gone mad,

        doused raindrop-gal screaming wild,

                became a blowjob-in-a-stairwell child.

Sixteen, Aching For Life

Juan, grown with two kids of his own,
wooed me into a nervous swoon.
I let him kiss me in parked cars. We necked
hours, his hands cupping my breasts.
He started to penetrate
when I let him lay me down under a tree,

but I screamed, *Take it out*, so loud
he obeyed, left me pulsing, vacant.
Our kisses stopped. He took me home
to Mama. She called me a slut.
Any good girl wouldn't be out past midnight.

Holding Onto Her Past

She is lost wanting familiar.
Tomorrow the rains may start, but this
is always the day before in her perpetual
quest. She holds a locket with a picture,
a small girl smiles, wears a cameo.
The 3 x 5 index cards she keeps
her best ideas on are lost. Misplacement
plagues her. Nothing ever reappears
once lost. The dense territory in her brain
a fog she cannot see through, like the ship
on the horizon the Indians did not notice.
The girl in the locket has scarred red blotches
grown the full length of her face
down her neck. She sits peaceful a tear
runs down one cheek, she asks,
what are you doing with such pure
skin, how will you use it?

Girls Like Her

I had not a clue of girls like her,
long fingers, long legs, Breck-blond silk against pale,
willing to explode my life for her.
Followed her and two boys into their hack radio station.

Her long fingers, long legs, Breck-blond silk against pale—
I dedicated my favorite song, *Spooky*, out into the airwaves.
Two boys in their hack radio station played *Spooky*—
cutting school, training into Manhattan, Central Park.

Dedicated to her, *Spooky*, played the airwaves.
Hours we drifted, fluid on the lake in a rowboat.
Cutting school, learning the trains, we traveled into Manhattan—
a search for Zackery, the man she intended to marry her mother.

Hours drifting fluid, rental boats we found in Central Park.
In her bedroom we shared secrets and dreams—
how the search for Zack would answer her prayers.
There I caught her, amenable to my kisses.

In her bedroom where we shared secrets and dreams,
always willing to explode my life for her,
rare moments amenable to my kisses,
I had not a clue of girls like her.

Love Fest On Bleecker Street

1
She had the blondest—
I followed her like a puppy,
at Forest Park her long legs

dangled from trees.
Let me kiss you, I whispered.
I cornered her in her bed

moved my mouth into her
gum-sweetened lips
we lay breast to breast

like a lotus on water
I love you, I said
but it was the 60s.

2
My first loss of innocence sweet.
I ate raisins off her tongue.

We wore bell-bottoms before the fray,
those years, like an ache unsatisfied
jumping out of a window was not the answer.

We bled at the same time, but
we grew apart. She said, *No,*
firmly, more assertive than ever,
engaged to the trophy man
between her legs.

3
Long weekend love fest,
hours wandering Washington Square
groovin' to a cappella,
amplified dreams of escape

sweet-meat we walked a marijuana haze,
our bell-bottoms ripped at the edges.

The call to sex repeats
        the constant drive
beating in the loins
        a bookmark between pages.

4
I wore that burgundy bridesmaid dress
stood at the altar, sang praise—
the world around us dense with mists of
wedding cake sweetness.

My tears, not for her blissful future.
She married the bastard who kissed me
        with hot lips
the night before they said, *I do*.

My reputation fixed,
she rode the train
respect.

Section II

Female Festers

Poetry is the opening and closing of a door, leaving those who look through to guess about what was seen during a moment.
—*Carl Sandberg*

Anything, To Take Away the Pain

> It would be very good if we would wake before we die.
> —Old Hindu saying

We had to get drunk
'till my head made me scream,
I want to die, loud—
everyone wake the fuck up
share this misery.
We two stayed up all night,
wandered Village
streets in tattered jeans,
tie-dyed mirror decals,
platform shoes.

I painted those years on
like my best friend's fingernails,
three inches long and multicolored.
The attention we attracted,
lines of coke, black beauties, downers
coming into our hands—
our fingernails
ready to break.

Dawn came craving roast beef with mayo
on Wonder Bread, and orange soda.
Together on a grassy knoll we sat and ate
to weigh our stomachs down—
shield our heads against the pain.

Mama You Just Don't Know

I swim the pool of your past,
fit into your clothes, heavy
your story how you craved a
beer while pregnant with me
first time in your life you could
drink the stuff I never can.

The sparkle in my eye
is the sparkle in your eye
lost beneath the weight of
surface talk that bogs us down.

Don't you want to
know the real answers
straight from my own mouth?
I love that black boy.
Please don't run away.

I need you to hear
the stories of my life.
I can no longer talk about
the flowers in Maryland, or the
manicured lawns of Virginia's
plantations.

You talk as if I were still a child,
don't go out in the rain
without your rubbers,
be careful crossing streets,
don't get your hair wet.

You bring cheese cake, rich
and sweet, but we eat through
conflict.

Why can't you find questions
that meet me half way?
Where is the you wanting
to know what counts in my life?

I can't remember one
street you crossed to meet me.

What Can a Street Urchin Expect?

Stretched out on a mattress flat on the floor,
no sheets or anything, he lies in this boarded up,
Lower East Side tenement building bound to be razed.
Shirtless, he flashes a pensive look like he's been waiting
for me to arrive. I imagine he wants sex. It is cold.
The mattress is dirty. I stand staring, his hard-on
sticks out of his warms ups. His feet are
calloused and stained like coffee, ugly. Pardon me,
I whisper hoarsely like I imagine a camel would speak,
this space is dank with urine and fills me with paranoia.
I will not have sex with you, thank you. It's that simple,
I know you jerk off all day waiting for
street urchins like me to appear seeking shelter. What
do you have to offer me anyway? That cock of yours means
nothing. Beat it off if you need to but don't expect you'll plug
into this. I flash my tits bare under a big bulky sweatshirt
twist it up and down fast at him—he groans, Please, he
pulls out his cock, just show me I promise I won't touch.
I pull my shirt up and down across my nipples
the cold air chafes them tender to sore. He spurts. Can I go now?
Never, come rest. I fall to the mattress next to him spent,
he crosses his arm over me. I let him hold me, glide to
sleep feeling released. He's not so bad. He covers
me with a rough army blanket and spoons his body-warmth
across my back.

Abandonment To Pleasure

In my blond Afro wig   I'm not myself,
my legs spread around his shoulders,
my body enfolding his flesh.

    Hot, like when Juan primed me to wet and sloppy,
        still a virgin.
    Or when Ernie creamed me hot and wanton,
        but I said no.

But now   ripe fruit
I've fucked many men
        silently
until tonight
in this new persona,
in a house where no one will hear—
he spoils me to screams
ruins me forever to lovers
        with no edge for thunder.

Riding the wild tremors of repeating climax
with a man who knows exactly how to please—
his lightening bolt
surges my electric ripples
        into screams.

He draws me out with his demands:
    Do you like it?
        Tell me, do you like it?
Never so blatant in sex,
my *yes* small and rising,
        yes,
            yes,
    You like it?

>   *Tell me you like it—*
Yes.
>   Yes.
>   *Yes,*
>   I scream—
>   thunder shaken

every cell in capitulation.

Ideal Childhood Except For Hodgkin's Cancer

Things were not exactly perfect
after Dad hitchhiked across country during the war years
collecting postcards, married to Mom he took our family photos
in front of the house where the old man lived with the Magnolia tree.

After he hitchhiked cross-country in the war years,
he drove the whole family south to visit the Everglades.
Easter we stood for photos under the magnolia tree at the old man's house.
I was the star in the lens in front of Daddy's camera.

When we visited south we walked the paths of the everglades,
Daddy's break from shoveling snow from our driveway.
I smiled, a bright star in the lens of his camera,
my father with a man's skills: build, hunt, grow, tend.

His rare break from shoveling snow from our driveway.
I didn't know how little time we had
together to learn his skills: building, hunting, growing, tending.
He would never have deserted his family.

I didn't know how little time we had
looking through his yellowing postcards, our family photos.
He didn't mean to desert us
things were never exactly perfect.

One Of the Many

Janis Joplin's gruff voice screaming to the hordes,
I wanted to live in her screams.
We sat in your day-glow room plastered with posters of Hendrix
Bohemians and Beats barely passé.

I wanted to live in full-surround-scream—
Led Zeppelin, The Doors, in mad love with Morrison.
We basked in the Bohemian equivalent of our generation,
Life magazine photos of Haight-Ashbury

Led Zeppelin, The Doors. How I loved Jim Morrison,
ragged cut jeans, everything bright
reminiscent of photos in *Life* magazine.
We sat at Café Reggio, watched kids like us on MacDougal.

Ragged cut jeans, tie-died bright
world of runaways,
we sat in Café Reggio watching the natives
never wanting to go back to Queens.

This world of runaways,
your room plastered with posters of Hendrix.
We had to go back to Queens.
Like Janis Joplin we screamed, on the subway to the hordes.

The Other Side

My best friend never did get over the past.
Jimi died, she sobbed.
This lifetime eats us.
She OD'ed that night Hendrix died.

Jimi died, repeated through her sobs.
I envied her outside the high school circuit.
She OD'ed later that night Hendrix died.
I searched for her in my orange and black Indian dress,

followed her outside our high school circuit—
ripping-gut Led Zeppelin screams,
searching Village streets in a dress that rode my ass,
a place I was warned never to go.

Ripping-gut the screams of Janis, Led Zeppelin—
we moved like screams in subways,
this place, the Village, I was warned never to go.
Years later, I found her, living in the Village married to a cousin.

We moved, like Janis Joplin screams, in subways.
This lifetime eats us,
lost in the Village married to a cousin,
no longer best friends, both of us still not over the past.

And If There Is No God

I said, *Yes*, out loud.
Maybe, I whispered beneath my breath.
All I wanted was a friend.
But my only friend lived next door,
a Catholic—and she
wanted to marry God.
What kind of husband
would God make?

I said, *Yes*, out loud.
Maybe, I whispered beneath my breath.
All I wanted was a place to hide,
a way to get to know this city
time to learn how to crack
this new world—this four-corner
metropolis—Manhattan a star
in the distance.

I said, *Yes*, out loud.
Maybe, I whispered beneath my breath.
All I wanted was to lie under a tree.
I entered church like stepping onto a bus—
pews swarming with boys and girls
I barely remember.
I walked the aisle.
Is there really a God?

I said, *Yes*, out loud.
Maybe, I whispered beneath my breath.
All I wanted was a place to escape.
I attended Sunday school
like a bride who registers at Macy's
before her wedding.
Confirmed in a white dress,
the only corsage I've ever worn.

The Expert

He knew all the answers
and he told them slowly, one by one,
while walking on the boardwalk.
We watch lovers kiss in the sand.
He tells me kissing on a beach is one thing
but a marriage of black and white
could not last—this he is sure of.
Love and kisses differ from a lifelong commitment.
The world isn't ready for marriage
between people of different races.
The children need to be one or the other.

He had an old turquoise Dodge.
Its hood flew open first day out on a highway.
He never met a woman who could put up with him,
no wife, no children, he was a caregiver for his mother,
his grandmother, and me.
He was a breadwinner
and he died having never gone anywhere
except to the war.

Truant

Sophomore year
      we flattened pennies
           on old railroad tracks

Best friends
      we longed for lovers
           traded used boyfriends

Back in those
      no soap   no radio
           easy-over days

West Village
      full of color
           splashed us bright

Transformed
      into the graffiti-
           side of an IRT

How good a cappella
      sounds in a park   with
           sweet wine

Too brief
      this stretch
      waffled over warnings:
           finish school

Punishment
      a quick flip of the egg
      but our relish
           was green

best friend
> beauty
> > a charm

for this homely child
> black-light Day-Glo garbed
> > everyone looks good

to think
> she can be
> anything
> > she wants to be

That was then
> the clock ticking
> indiscriminate
> > against tie-dye

Wooed by Smokey
> *Oh Baby*
> and not one
> > deadline   to meet.

Ivory Coast Boy

invites me to do homework.
I like his smile
his music.
Who is he?

I kiss him
in our school hallway.
Girlfriends pout
eyes open wide,
promise not to tell.
Rumors spread.
I become tramp.
He becomes rapist.
We do homework together,
look into one another's eyes.
This is not who we are.

best friend
> beauty
>> a charm

for this homely child
> black-light Day-Glo garbed
>> everyone looks good

to think
> she can be
> anything
>> she wants to be

That was then
> the clock ticking
> indiscriminate
>> against tie-dye

Wooed by Smokey
> *Oh Baby*
> and not one
>> deadline   to meet.

Ivory Coast Boy

invites me to do homework.
I like his smile
his music.
Who is he?

I kiss him
in our school hallway.
Girlfriends pout
eyes open wide,
promise not to tell.
Rumors spread.
I become tramp.
He becomes rapist.
We do homework together,
look into one another's eyes.
This is not who we are.

Lessons From a Surrogate

I entered at the surface afraid—
a good Seagram's and ginger ale Uncle taught me.
I explored this world through one man's eyes—
Rockettes dancing, single women with long legs.

A good Seagram's and ginger ale, 7&7, he taught,
his martyr caregiver role growing me up fast.
Black & white photos, him paired with long legged women—
difficult years, still a child in penny loafers.

His caregiver martyr role growing me—
teen trouble acting out, tottering on too high heels.
Difficult years, still a child toting scratchy legs.
He walked me into steakhouses to show me the good life.

Through those troubled years acting out,
hung over in diners my eyes hungry met the eyes of men.
Walking into steakhouses he said, *a man will bring you here someday*.
Eating roast beef I eyed the counterculture, he spit warnings.

Hung over in diners, he told me, *never look a man in the eye*.
I explored this world though one man's eyes.
I ate roast beef watching the counterculture side—
always a new surface to enter afraid.

What Is Buried and Past

Mother turned Baptist
wanted me dunked.
Uncle visited the Lutheran church.
Both railed against the Catholics.
Neither ever mentioned Jew.

Confusions in this family—
visages closed
like a basement door
with a lost key and no need
to ever enter again.
The basement has a dirt
floor I've been told
years ago by a grandmother
long dead. Some jars
of canned food might still
be stored, probably full
of botulism. If we ever
did go down there,
it would be thrown
away. Mother and Uncle
insist we move on. Insistence
is the mode and there is no
looking back, no link to the
secrets buried with the key
to the basement, it's in their
stool passed long ago.

Pastoral Landscape

Did I really sit in the moonlight parked on a hill
overlooking my father's grave
while a hormonally-enraged male
manhandled me to near rape?
And did I really fall out of the car in climax
screaming, *No, I'm a virgin*, in full view
of my father's grave?

I was a daughter on her way to adulthood
where no father can save her.

Feral

I kicked him.
He let the old feral cat inside.
The neighbors hoarded cats.
They were used to the smell of dead rats,
the stench of death,
piss rotting every floor they walked on.

I didn't visit home often.
My uncle received a note from the son of the woman next door,
a card saying he thought they could be friends,
a card that broke ice,
a card with a cat on the cover, of course.
Against all better sense he knocked on the feral cat neighbor's door.
This is their life, I declared.
Then cat-mother, hair wild, a stub of a cigarette wrapped in her lips,
her teeth green, wandered in wanting to talk.
My mother welcomed her. *I cannot stay*, I said, looking into feral eyes.
I cannot stay for the smell, it is not personal.
I ran upstairs, tears at what my family was coming to.
Next, the feral cat-mother was sleeping between my clean sheets,
the middle of the night in my clean sheets.
A feral cat ran through my bare legs in the hall
on the way to the bathroom.
My mother's eyes turned, she pulled out a cigarette
though she'd never smoked before.
Don't expose me to second hand smoke, my best scientific jargon.
She snuffed it out in the hem of her dress pushing against the sideboard.
Middle of the night and nowhere to go,
feral cat woman between my sheets,
my last night ever in this house,
sinewy hopes and dreams caught in the thick ropey muscle of cat.
One forgets essentials in a feral home, it is a wonder to stay clean.
Stench through my pores turns me out wild.

Myths Of Difference

> "skin crazy, but I'm trying
> to get some other eyes, you know—"
> –after Tim Seibles

the damage one does   oneself
         feeling so alive

I went to Sly concerts
at least eight times   cried
when he married   live on stage

at Madison Square   took Mom's
money   snuck out the house
         to scream wild

a place to see   black & white
together   no one knew
where their daughter-child flew

skin-crazy back in Queens
I sought   other eyes
let The Doors   explode me blind

Jim Morrison's   shrill guitar
his blood   curdling   screams

pierced my heart   my hands turned black
n'blue   internal bleeding   from so much
         applause

Infatuation

He sat calm over espresso
A hotshot opaque black man
Watching the parade of hippies pass by
Rings on his fingers, his shoes perfectly shined

A hotshot opaque black man
His nails manicured long
Gold rings shining off his fingers, his shoes buffed
My best friend dated his best friend, she fixed us up

His long fingernails manicured with gold polish
He and his friend lived in hotels
My best friend fixed us up
We went to movies: *Shaft, Putney Swope, Butch Cassidy*

He and his friend lived in hotels
Mom swore I'd wind up poor living in a ghetto
He took me to movies: *Shaft, Putney Swope,* that *Sundance Kid*
Did the fine white powder drugs, different than friendly pot

Mom swore I'd wind up in a ghetto with a black child, alone
I sat with him watching the parade of hippies walk by
We'd snorted the fine white powder, so different from pot
When I broke up, he sat calm over espresso

Freak

some people call him
when he isn't looking. They smile
to his face, think he can't see them
out of his pink-hazel albino eyes.
Always, he wears a hat, his fro
white kinky at the edges. He shaves
short but not bald, lets his hair
top-tall, keeps it tight in back. His
pale skin pocked with acne
he's slowly growing out of.
Can't be easy growing up white
in his black world. He lives his
tall self out of a low back-throat
whisper like Isaac Hayes swoons.
When he speaks, the crowd slows
and listens. He dates my best friend,
so he grows normal to my eyes.
When she's done with him, it
doesn't seem unnatural to get with him,
so I'm dating a freak. Already crossed
the black boundary. What's one more?
A good man, he works hard,
keeps the books for a small porn
company in Manhattan, gets us free
passes to films. I tell him, *Let's
find the ones with plots*. And we do.

Chevy Impala '60

We drive north.
    It's thirty degrees in daylight
        minus ten by midnight.

Blankets wrapped around us,
    the heater in this old Chevy
        stopped working years ago.

I your driver,
    you, legally-blind,
        wanted this trip

north
    NYC to the Adirondacks.

The driver's side door
    jammed tight
I crawl over you each rest stop
    crazy in jeans you
        grab my breasts.

Your black-albino features
    stark against snow
        hazel-pink eyes.

We speed too fast
    skid the plowed highways

make our way cold
    into colder.
        The radio won't work.

A cooler in the trunk
    with eggs and frozen chuck.
        A cabin waits
            fires to be built
                icicles to melt.

Breakfast Special

It was our weekend morning diner.
The one half-way between here
and there, our routine meeting place
for breakfast. The same frizzed
blond, her hair tight in a bun
with a net, an apron to wipe
her hands. *How you doing,
Hon? Same?* And yes, we had the same.
Eggs and toast. Coffee. You lit my
cigarette, held my hand. Here
we felt safe from the jeers your
albino features raised on the streets.
We had fights, shed tears
over the remaining god-awful
frozen potato hash I never finished.
And celebrations, like the time
we finished shopping for our kitchen
on Delancey. Got the best bargain
ever that Sunday morning, butcher block
with a separate base dusty from the back
of the store. A steal deal. But today
I come alone. You've left me, I cry
on the red cushioned seat staring
out the door like you'll walk in
any second. But nothing. Except
the waitress, who asks, *Where's your
grandfather, Hon?* My mouth falls
into the ashes on my cigarette,
Grandfather! The stupidity of diners
falls on me like pigeon shit, I smile, say,
I'll take the shame, she doesn't see,
doesn't hear. My diner days
are done.

Sunday Morning

The bicycle with threadbare
tires rests in the shadowed
hallway. I make apple pies,
climb the back stairway
to our bed of quilted squares
knit to keep us warm.

Recipes I bake in our oven,
quiche, frittatas. I serve you
breakfast in bed, lounge
curled into your curves.
We read each other our writing
plan books we want to write,

my hands soothe your warm body,
I feed you my time.

Union

There is a crossing
always, a threshold
someone carries someone over
a woman in a long white dress,
a ring on her finger.

Alive as the night
passionate as the wind
blowing the door closed,
trembling into his arms.
His fingers fumble,
pushing her miniature pearl
buttons, looking for the loop.

Now the gown falls with its satin-
heavy thrust, her skin glows pink
against his palm flat, white
tracing her bones.

His breath moves her
to whisper in their bed.
Across the room, another
doorway opens to a cave
where lions sleep, open their eyes
yawn and stretch, watching. He has them
under perfect control.

Dangerous to play with,
their eyes milky, half awake.

She'll make bouquets of weeds,
stinging nettles in full height
with their green seeds drooping,
amaranth heavy with red kernels,
lacy angelica. They'll form a team.
She's protected in these wilds
with her man.

He eats her on the bed, her cake and icing
he takes his fill, quenches his thirst
he, heavy with lion, holds her
beyond how men hold women.

So it is up to her
to feed his lions and smile,
let her dress fall to the floor,
open the door, let the wind close it again,
watch time close around them.

She needs milk and cheese
and the nibbling life of the senses.
When she brings
her first goat through their door
he tells the lions
not to kill.

Paint Job

I let myself be painted once
why not I reasoned, done everything else
let them smear body paint all over my breasts
she was my best friend
he was her lover of the moment
could be fun.

I remember the feel of the brush
pig hair with long dark bristles
then the fingers, I leaned back
in the backseat of his daddy's Lincoln
parked somewhere deserted near Rockaway
it was August hot
I closed my eyes sank into the wheat-grain leather between them
naked from my waist up, pants unzipped
their eyes flirted across me, their playland
he asked if I'd ever exchanged sex
for money, no I said
I'm not a whore
just a slut.

Primary colors
crude flower designs around each nipple
their fingers moved slow
a small tug to my nipple
to get the colors just right
giggling they begin to run details
vines and leaves down my stomach
I laughed with them
awkward, excited, wondering how I looked
knowing my breasts were what they wanted.

I fantasize my fingers dipped in paint
winding vines and leaves closer and closer
to her private parts as they moved towards mine.

It all stopped
no one was sure
          what came next
there was some diddling with his cock
but we had no road map for three way turns
she really didn't want me with her man
she only wanted to amuse him.

So it was with the friend
I used to do anything for.

Catalyst To Manhattan

He was my catalyst, introducing me to his Manhattan,
Knew every back alley, down a flight of stairs restaurant in Chinatown
Took me to Kung Fu movies, then we ate snails in black bean sauce
I drank plum wine, he ordered native speaking in Korean haunts

He knew back alley downstairs restaurants hidden in Chinatown
The night we met he took me to an after hours jazz joint
Turned on to him and plum wine at his favorite Korean haunt
I learned to love hum bow, sushi and kimchee

We left that after hours joint smiling in bright sunlight
Tae Kwon Do black belt, he invited me to take classes
After workouts, we noshed on sushi, hum bow, or kimchee
High kick workout-sweat sessions, he was a strict teacher

Tae Kwon Do black belt master, I loved his classes
Over mussels in white wine he handed me a Tiffany blue box
Sweat dry on my brow proud of my earned yellow belt
He slid a friendship ring on my right index finger

Our favorite fish joint, his gift, a friendship ring from Tiffany
In love with Kung Fu movies, snails in black bean sauce
His ring a permanent fixture on my finger
He was my catalyst out of Queens finally to Manhattan

A Good Arrangement

Good at keeping secrets.
Good at telling lies.
Done with my slut phase,
hours spent necking with married men who didn't care
about much else but getting in my pants.
They had wives and mistresses and took me on the side.
Done with lust coming at me—
settle down with one man,
I had a good one,
ready to give me a ring.

Then, you walked into that shabby clinic,
that prefab building with its cut up office cubes,
sitting lonely on a far block in Rockaway.
I was a lab technician.
You were an intern,
a neurosurgeon standing Greek statuesque,
a square jaw,
bronze skin
chestnut hair you could barely keep out of your eyes.
You were temporary, time restrained,
a one year internship.
I went berserk calculating
the calendar months before you would move away.

That old cliché, love at first sight,
stung me a main line injection of belief
there was no antidote for.
My slut relapsed.
You were married with a child,
it was my turn not to care.
I put that kid miles out of my mind.
Ready to fall into you,
my hand grazed your knee.
It was up to you to figure out where and when and how.
Those who keep secrets know there is always a way.
I had no place of my own.

No privacy. I lived with parents.
It was back then,
had to be male prerogative.
You made a plan.
I would travel to the VA in St. Albans
on your overnight shifts.
There was a room with a cot and you had a key.
It was always late, I was buzzed in at the gate.
We had a place to whisper quiet,
a place to nuzzle.

Our arrangement—
never interfere with your marriage,
a promise I made.
This was what love was meant to be.
No demands.
You were always to return to Boston.
We went to no motels,
exchanged no gifts,
made no future commitment.
I called you Doctor,
used your last name.
It made the secret easier to maintain.
Made our eyes dance a conspiracy at work.

I was wet between my thighs
and wearing an engagement ring from my steady.
Does it feel heavy?
No, I said sincere,
but the wonder at your question stuck.
The wedding plans grew too expensive.
The future mother-in-law invited relatives I didn't know.
I strategized, said to my fiancé,
Let's buy a car instead.
My fiancé kept asking what was wrong.
After you left, Rockaway Beach waves swallowed me.
The ring weight pulled me under.

Smell Of Mother

There is a smell that reminds me of Mother.
It drifts from between warm thighs
opened in heated bathrooms where privacy
begs forgiveness on warm nights.

Certain skirts hold that smell
and basins in kitchen sinks forever try
to wash it away—it is a woman's smell
the essence of Mother.

Occasionally a whiff knocks me down,
when I encounter it somewhere
unexpected, a public restroom,
a woman on a plane stands suddenly

to search the overhead,
the natural musk I travel to escape.

Section III
Woman Stands

Expose yourself to your deepest fear; after that, fear has no power, and the fear of freedom shrinks and vanishes. You are free.
—*Jim Morrison*

Pushed Edges: Lovemap Explorations

"The lovemap may manifest itself also in masturbation fantasies or in daydreams and reveries with or without culminating to orgasm."
>*The Lovemap Guidebook A Definitive Statement*
>by John Money

I play games
free-fall
      alter-ego games

Each lover
a notch
in my thirst
to feel
to heal

I am—vixen, slut, goddess, whore

1.
      I put on

           a blond afro wig

kneel to suck a lean clean-cut cock
my moans echo under the stairwell—
we wait for the bus—
      his hand firm
           presses the back of my neck
his voice deep
      suck it good

2.
      At the beach

           in only a trench coat

my breasts bare—nipples pulled hard
pinned against a brick wall
    prostitute pick-up scene
        he pays cash

3.
    In short-shorts I lick clean

        my ice cream cone

wet fuck in the back of his Dodge
parked at Dairy Queen
    I scream *rape*
my wrists roped to the door—thighs wild
what I want—don't want—
        the boys outside

4.
    Summer retreat

        where I chance to meet

divorced PTSD Viet Nam vet
    mercy fuck
he wants me so bad
    wants to fuck me hard

please—please—
I give him
    my thirst
        all my cathartic thirst

Spice Rack

Cooking with Coral—
lamb chops marinated with garlic and lemon,
I reach for her spices—dusty, drippy—
What is with these spices?
How old are they?
My questions, my compulsive need
      to clean her spice corner,
          wash each of her glass jars.

She calls it my nesting instinct.
I want to be with her
want her house clean, deep clean.
Clean spice jars a view
to how open her heart is.

I wipe them down—
will not let them sit
all greasy and soiled.
Deep cleaning takes time
soothing to the soul time.

A kitchen must be clean at the start,
every pot, every burner ready
and there must be spices
fresh, fragrant in clean jars
not stale, dried out old spices.

Love will come when a kitchen is un-crusted.
Clean and ready for a game of pool—
brussel sprouts shot across her table.
When it is ready, we will enfold soft butter
in layers of phyllo dough
use poppy seed filling, licking finger good.
When it is ready, we will squish bread
with mushrooms and sausage

use fresh tarragon, dill and rosemary
slide it easy into the cavity of a raw bird.

In her kitchen
cooking up love
we indulge in red meat lamb.

Hot Woman

You have this hot woman in the car next to you, humming herself into masturbation. Her fingers ready to submerge. Just keep driving. Don't veer your eyes from the road, cause an accident. There is no one around to see. This is the American male dream come true. Lucky tonight. Hot time fire tonight. She wants you to know everything will be all right. It is in her skin. Smooth and silky like a baby's ass. You both remember. That is why she creams. The car smells musk. Breathe in funky perfumed essence of woman. Woman not girl. You've had girls before. They are different to smell. They are powder caked on. Douches that cleanse away taste. They are afraid of smell and crust. This is a woman who has mucus that will not wait. Her fumes mix with the gas. High octane that screams loud in the wind. You slow down for her, pace yourself, open your chest, her whim is your desire tonight on back roads. Coyotes howl knowing she's in heat in the back of your car in a field where the moon is bright and her dress is up to her ears over her head without worry of wrinkles. She has no barriers, no hesitations. She is not the city girl you left in the bedroom who couldn't say yes, who wanted to but didn't, who had no context for passion. That girl was a book, an encyclopedia you loved for a thesis. This woman is the cow in the barn wanting to be milked. This woman is falling into your arms no words to distract, only the guttural sounds from the back of her throat, the screams that have no accent of particular pronunciation. She is body and sound bound into skin and bone, her crevices aching to be full of your full gut roar.

She may never come here again. She will pass on to her next lover. Call once a year to see if you are well.

I. Safety Fable

She finds herself   alone   walking   2:30 am   west to
east   underground   beneath 42ⁿᵈ St   a deserted
white tile tunnel   her footsteps echo   the long stretch
empty   her bubble breaks   alone   click   click   her
heels echo   break   the eerie underground silence
she gathers herself   commands her fear: go away   the walls watch
click   click step-by-step   she will not stop   nor freeze
into panic   she swallows: calls on her wolves   they fill the
white tunnel yapping   she catches the number 6   she travels
home   this underground maze, unnatural   a woman   dressed
in heels, click, click,   click, on concrete,   independent   going
home   on a subway, never a cab budget   public transportation
chick   she might have   taken a bus   stayed above ground
if she   realized the hour,   remembered the long maze, but she did
what she always did   alone   alert   she has wolves
to call on.

II. Beyond the School for Wayward Girls

Some indecent exposure does no harm   when she goes
her boundaries set at half mast: only she can set   the touch
don't touch   distinction   maybe she wants stray hands to study
her cervix   to teach her secrets   she'd never know   behind
walls   let her go   to freedom   to scarves   to sing her
song with musicians   play out   her groupie dreams
her face a still life   her lips a flower shade of pale   Her
accounts: Her yes. Her no.   her eyes spew gold
       her hands radiate   her feet bare on the earth
her womb gathers storms   her being   a beacon   a path
she must follow   guided from inside

78

III. Jesus Tossed The Dice

Their worst fears: white slavery, death, destitution, murder, bound and gagged in a dungeon, stuck with a black child in a ghetto, drug addict lying in a corner in a crack house selling herself for a hit, sleeping in a doorway in winter, kidnapped in a trunk, raped and strangled to death, cut up body parts in the Green River, strung up dead from erotic asphyxiation.

Hell no   she'll tiptoe   fly high   rise to the occasion
take the stage   dance   sing   laugh   hold court   serve tea
dapple with drugs   disco at Danceteria   play gay   dress
up   walk miles   cruise   and yes   bruise: 18, 18, 18
free at 18   free   to go   she will go   she goes   no
more walls   no gate   freedom   to do what she will
be who she must be   create what she needs   this storm of
her life   this tornado

One End To the Other

Gut-words rise from my intestines full of fire—
saffron-loaded pistils, spice I never knew as a child.

One of the many adult indulgences, stuffed olives with pimentos.
Artichokes, how one lays the leaf on the tongue, uses the teeth

to extract life, the pliable foundation of a journey with attitude
spitfire at the brim. I stuck out my tongue, balled my fists

in the street where the food got down and dirty—Orange Julius
with a raw egg for breakfast was healthy, a way to bend morning

inside out on 8th Street walking one end to the other—St. Marks
to the call of egg creams, then blow off with a hot dog on 6th Avenue.

Now Manhattan's one health food store after another, and teens
stand outside the doors high on crack. The LSD days flew

Air West outta here. Psychedelic minds didn't want food—
the face in the mirror was enough to absorb those endless days.

Come on, play that Sly album one more time—
his wedding concert where mourning, I fired up a duby.

St. Mark's Place Brother

Blond actor I adopt sits over papers
pen-in-hand. His Arabic painted table
between us, gift from his Egyptian lover,

a reminder of my regret—I missed Egypt
for lack of funds, but the dancing never
stops, and home-grown rests easy

in his pouch for hand-rolled. Masters,
we role-play, he paces, *Yes, Yes, Yes.*
We pitch a drug treatment center. Plan to

display paths, stepping stones
to make life work. In his St. Marks Place
five-floor walk-up, we eat roast chicken—

every color on the plate makes a perfect
meal. I help move his freebee TV,
gasp up those stairs. Water his plants.

Keep his keys, his home my home.
Uptown downtown we share.
His face on Broadway. Greta

Garbo walks my Upper East Side
quiet along the river in gray. Come
Christmas, sis visits, we bake,

make 2 am runs for butter, sugar.
All the girls want my brother now—
he wants the leading actor, dreamy-

eyed like I've never seen him.
Tilted against his fireplace—
hair dyed black for the role,

Directors' prefer dark hair, he says.
Blond better, like yellow peppers
coloring the plate next to red beets,
collard greens, organic chicken.

Friends, together we make it.

Snared

disco nights   full blare blast sound   under black light
glass globes   circle endless   we blink secret codes

captured   in the dance   we play
weave through the crowd   disco grove   our fingers linked

single file   you follow   we dance   dance   dance
spiral upstairs to the balcony   above the bar   stare at the big picture

our musical pause   we lean on the rail   pulse in our touch
I fall into you   a female colorful bird   who's picked her mate

from the crowd   you at the end of my snare   chosen
we dance   dance   dance

Donna Summers   our witness   moans our love song
we sing our vows   *Love to love you baby*   *Love to love you baby*

if you leave   stop the dance   change the rules
I will follow you   we are two   who snared   who

Meant To Be

We could have met
no later, no earlier
our accidental clocks
set in the stars
or the planets—
the whole universe
came together
an exact series of
calculations
fate.

Our caldrons brewing
each of us doing our work—
you in your world
preparing:
> clearing out a dresser drawer
> making space in your closet,
> finding a double bed.

Practical steps to move
from bachelorhood to partnership.

All that inner work:
coaxing yourself from shy,
learning to dance,
attending events women love,
drawing in art therapy classes,
exploring demons in dream circles.

You cut away baggage
no future mate could want.
Had a dad who grew old into a house
piled ground to sky—
he died alone on top of newspapers,
magazines, guns, toolboxes, unopened
CD's, charcoal in decaying bags.

On a bushwhacking trip through Maine
I carried the I Ching
questioned if I was gay or bi—
I was everything
haphazard as the winds of lust
sex uncontained
longing for a father
to save me.

What Uncle and Mother could never
give in their crazy house in Queens—
      falling down roof
        burnt out electric circuits
        no washing machine
        no shower.

Each of us walked a long path back.
Intrigued by a sound growing inside
like my father's whistles.
That night you led me
onto the dance floor
something sparked,
we began.

My Brave Lynx

He says he has something to ask me.
What, I say, open to anything.
I think to myself, *This is my man.*
He pauses, asks, *What if I stop working,
live off the race track for a year?*

Horse races?
He's been lucky at the track.
Exactly. We stand face to face—
        I see horses in his eyes.

New York streets quiet around us—
Sixth Ave, a groomed dirt
bed, a distant church bell
        chimes across town.
You think you can do that?
Lynx-certain he replies, *I'm good at it.*
Horses come around the curve
        at the base of Manhattan.
Why not, I say, *It's your life.*
His arms soft
        surround me in a hug.

We snap back cross Sixth Ave
        after the last horse
               passes the finish line.

Salvatore's

We walk there in jeans,
a quiet neighborhood stroll after a headache day,
seeking the comfort pasta offers, an easy table
in a corner to unwind. We are seated
by a window after a short wait.

It's a packed house, our eyes adjust
to the glow of candles. Young women
in gowns giggle and clutch their wine
glasses. Adolescent men wear rented tuxes,
bury their noses into their date's corsage,
desire the sweet skin beneath.
It must be prom night.

We'd laughed about this being Seattle—
fleece city, how even the most expensive
restaurants are casual. I'd joked,
I doubt there will be strapless gowns.
Yet here we sit on a June night in a restaurant
full-tabled with women in gowns, feather
boas draped lusciously around their necks.
Limos wait outside.

We're careful to order within our budget,
avoid the simple fare we can make at home.
Waiters scurry with full trays of appetizers,
refills of wine, giggles grow louder. We nurse
sips from our glasses, my pea and tarragon ravioli
melted heaven in a puff. Our tradition, we trade
plates, taste each other's food. His lasagna
a miracle. How long since we made our best lasagna.
It takes time to slow down for such perfection.

Youth squeals to have photos taken, waiters
rush to their service, cluster them to fill the frame,
blinding lights like a flashback comes the prom
I never attended, a suitor turned down long ago
in a different age, back when I didn't know
what a relationship could mean. Across the table
a man I've lived with a quarter of a century,
who like me, missed his senior prom.
We refuse dessert, we don't drink coffee.
We'll have our sweets at home.

Love Transformations

1.
You are a bird dancing. I am
a solid wood dresser—long missing
linseed oil penetration.

You are the wild nettles growing,
wanting to feed iron to the masses
walking by. Let me be the one
who stops and let health
impose upon my body. And we
the dance composed that takes
this world by storm.

2.
You are a rose quartz gem in a
medicine pouch. I am a wanderer
lost in a maze.

You are the plums growing
without tending along the river.
Let me harvest the fruit you bear
and you shine the lightness from
losing your burden. Let us dance
and lightened disappear forever.

3.
You are a well-read book. I am
an octopus converted to land.

You are deadly nightshade, your
red berries climb the stairwell
banister glistening in the sun. Let
me be sun warming you and you
the poison leached from my body,
exiting, and we flying together in
fall winds.

4.
You are a screen door—keeping flies
out. I am a boa constrictor with no
one to hug.

You are the wheat unharvested
in a two hundred square foot plot, with no
sun. Let me be the sunlight that warms
you, and you the seed that grows
in my body, harvested, and we
the bread unheated and day old.

5.
You are a turquoise scarf woven in
Mexico. I am a small poisonous frog
from the depths of Africa.

You are a magic carpet flying
ancient city to modern world in
some time machine. Let me ride
your golden threads, carry the time
piece, and you the lint in my belly-
button, and we pollinate in a far
and distant land.

6.
You are a little boy lost and alone. I am
a pear ripe on a tree.

You are seaweed tangled in the ocean
flowing with each wave. Let me be the incoming
tide to gently rock you and you a song
serenading, and we a chant that never
ends.

7.
You are a La-Z-Boy chair reclined and
empty. I am the ice in a glass of cranberry
juice.

You are slippers worn around the edges.
Let me be the soft comfort and you
the toes within wiggling free, and we
toasty warm on a long walk.

8.
You are an organizing file, alphabetical.
I am a Frieda Kahlo painting hanging
at the Met.

You are a racecar driver coming
in first on a slippery track. Let me
be the slippery track you slide along
to first place, and you the screech
crossing the finish line, and together we win.

9.
You are Blaxploitation watching
all the films. I am color blind, see
only with deaf eyes.

You are an honest chef preparing
breakfast over easy. Let me
be the morning rising you
to welcome each day, and you the kiss
I start my day with, and we the two
who sit face to face
for two meals each day.

10.
You are organic roasted hazelnuts
waiting to be eaten. I am fresh coffee,
bagged, sitting on a shelf.

The Only Thing Left

I finger brightly colored
lanyard bracelets Daddy
made in the war. He wove
to pass the time,
then brought them home
to Mom.

Passed on now
to me, broad weavings,
they bend to fit my arm.

I touch red, green, gold,
blue, think of Daddy's smile.
How he whistled
working wood at his bench
in the basement.

Birthday Reflection

It is my dead uncle's birthday.
Every year I remember
his birthday, precursor to my father's birthday
       and to my father's death.
             The men in my life.

I sit eating squid in Korean hot sauce,
kimchee and miso soup. My lips burn.
Going out with Uncle for pizza
         or clams on the half-shell
I had no idea the wide varieties of food
        I would meet.

My new man arrives to join me,
helps me finish the abundance of heat.

All I Want

is an open road, an easy fall
into soft grass, sun warming my skin
to freckles. Let me sleep late
between 400-count sheets, eat
strawberry ice cream, talk
of Socrates, sing goddess chants
with morning pancakes.

I love how we sat in a teepee
peeling pomegranates, sharing stories.
How we snap wishbones to decide.

On our lanai, you peel the brown skin
from devil's club branches, expose
the sacred clasped hands the Native tribes
revere. Its deep earth scent permeates
our living space.

May we always have Broadway tunes
on our tongues, dance steps bending our knees.
Let me have the rusty license plates
from our last car, mountains we climb
to make love, your breath in my ear.

I want a day not on the calendar
a minute devoid of tomorrow.
Let us sit peeling walnuts across the table.
Make a list, careful,
each minute counts.

Hot Days Of Past

Whipper-snapper men
lodged inside my cells.

I feel my insides jar
when I walk street-side
my attention drawn
to some random brown-skinned
muscle-backed construction crew
hard-hat big-boy who lounges—
his foot resting easy behind him
poised against a brick wall—
knee skin peeks out ripped
jeans. I walk by, fifty-frump,
fractured mid-line, my feet sport
easy-clogs.

Yearn for Danny Boy, back in Queens,
me in my short-short skirt
halter top—hot pink with mirror decals—
34C bouncing—bra-free, Danny Boy
making moves on me. My clit
at attention, I walk spiked heels
show-down.

Today's eye-candy
looks to some young chick
clad in spandex, she's Chinese,
carries a lunch box—
my back-there-then-self
says, if only it were then-here-now
and he, a simulated Danny Boy,
looking beyond middle-age
eyeballing-me-down.

Cupcake

He's a cupcake, one of those
Father's Day specials—chocolate
with caramel drizzle across the top.
Yum. Can't help but equate men with food,
what new restaurant to try next,
but dream cupcakes are only figments—
small bites that walk away into sunsets
settling their baseball caps.

Romantic, eating in candlelight
across from the one who always shows.
It's not true there's one man for every woman—
Adam and Eve only a metaphor—double
equations don't work outside of math.
But somehow I found that one man
in a complex formula where chemistry
and heat equal alchemy.
He's delicious.

A Family Visit

deep in the darkness
of the red-velvet wallpapered room
with its dark-red rug that shows no dirt,
sunlight dim through maroon curtains
we congregate, Mother intent
on pushing food into our face,
Uncle heavy in his chair,
reading glasses on the edge of his nose
a crossword puzzle in hand.
Sis paces by the mahogany sideboard.
Older sister visits from out of town.
They congregate in the darkening room.

Dried out wallpaper hangs off the wall
frayed and yellowed. Pull it down, burn it.
Curtains, shabby, dense with grease,
yank them from the windows, let the light in,
dust the chandelier, replace the dead light bulbs.
That moldy rug, spotted and worn where mites dance
and cats piss, pull it from the floor
take it to the dump.

Mother needs a new dress,
Uncle a long walk.
Hose out the refrigerator,
polish the mahogany.
That faded mountain fire-yellow sunset painting
replace it with Grandmother's mirror
dusty in the basement.
Paint the walls a soft cream.
Put breezy white curtains on the windows.
Bring in the sunlight, exit the doom.

She tries to do the dishes,
dreams herself a whirling force of change.

Fruit Fly Song

ice cream sits in a freezer
a fly sits on the wall
even in the densest story

Daddy died, the fly unnoticed

we faced each other
he was all I saw at my eleven

no flies on the wall
no ice cream cravings
my belly sank

something, anything,
but his flesh flat against his skull
his skin, like his hospital gown
like the white walls tinted green-gray

I worry about fruit fly season
how I will keep my kitchen clean

fruit flies laugh themselves free
from our joke, the flytrap
tiny whining voices scream
their songs of freedom
wiggle, determined, to the edge
insist their right to live full lives

Family Endurance

It is old, antique,
our grandmother's stole,
muskrat, with soft stripes,
a wrap for over her shoulders,
silky, I pet my grandmother.
She sits in my closet—

encased in a garment bag,
moved across country with me.
Grandfather's gift to Myrtle—
sleek and fashionable
to wear to the opera.
He, a composer, played piano

in our parlor every holiday.
Gave a piano, his dream gift,
to our mother for her wedding.
Piano lessons our family mantra.
Grandfather kept his job, kept food
on the table, they survived hard times.

My sister gave me the stole
she kept Grandmother's diamond ring—
our only keepsakes, assets
we prepare to sell as recession swells—
this the opera my sister and I sing.
I place an ad, go to a consignment shop,

am told, no one buys fur anymore
in the Northwest, it's politically incorrect.
I walk through the racks my hand
glides one fur to the next feeling
the shoulders, such soft ancestors
who've traveled centuries.

Ice Storm, Early 1950s

I stand in a snowsuit
safe in a white tunnel.
My front yard pathway
a wall of snow piled high
above my head.

Two large pines tower
over me, offering green,
crisp blue sky is far away.
Daddy shovels. School is
closed. Daddy cannot

go to work. I help him
shovel. Mother waits inside
with hot chocolate, she stands
where heat blows through the
metal grate from the coal fire

furnace. My hand, dry
in its glove touches the wall
of snow. Warm, sweat locked
inside, bundled against
the cold helping Daddy.

About the Author

Julene Tripp Weaver received her Bachelors in creative writing from the City University of New York, where she studied with Audre Lorde. Since moving to Seattle, she received a Masters in Applied Behavioral Science from the Leadership Institute of Seattle. She worked in HIV/AIDS services for 18 years before starting a private counseling practice. *Finishing Line Press* published her chapbook *Case Walking: An AIDS Case Manager Wails her Blues*, from which a poem was featured on *The Writer's Almanac*. Her poems are published in many journals, including *Main Street Rag, The Healing Muse, Knock, Arabesques Review, Nerve Cowboy, Crab Creek Review, Qarrtsiluni, Hot Metal Press, Gemini Magazine, Chicken Pinata, Outward Link, Blossombones, The Smoking Poet, Drash,* and *Future Earth Magazine;* and the anthology, *A Dream in the Clouds,* featuring art inspired by the 2008 Presidential Election. She does word play on Twitter @ trippweavepoet, and you can find more of her writing on her website: www.julenetrippweaver.com.

Photo by John Perkins

Breinigsville, PA USA
03 March 2011

256853BV00002B/1/P